Social Media Guide for Small Business

Market Your Products & Services via FB Fan Pages, FB Ads, Twitter & Instagram

Ethan Adams

Contents

Introduction

In this short book you will get a step by step instruction on how to go from zero fans on Facebook (and no fan page) to having your first 1,000 active followers.

If you're a beginner with Facebook marketing, then this book is for you. If you already have lots of experience when it comes to FB fan page marketing, then just throw this book away, now!

If you're a local business owner or a small business owner of some kind, then this book is also for you.

Now, if you don't have any business yet, then this book won't do you any good.

Yes, you can start learning this now but if you have no plans on starting a business anyway, then this book won't be of any value to you.

I just want to be honest with you.

Since this book would be 99% actionable content, you'll only benefit from reading it if you already have some sort of service or product to sell.

That said, I will try my best to make this as short and concise as possible,

I want you to spend more time taking action than reading. Let's dive into it.

Chapter 1 — Fan Page Creation

Here's how you'll create a fan page.

Hover to the right side of your account. Click the settings part.

And then click Create Page.

The next step is to choose your own category. Don't take this lightly.

Make sure that you have the right category for your own products or services.

Let us assume that you have a BBQ RESTAURANT.

Put the complete details of your business and click Get Started.

The next step is to complete the info needed.

Make your description short and straight to the point. What is it that you offer?

Tell em.

PROFILE PICTURE

For your profile picture, make sure that you have an hd picture with your service or product in action.

Here are some examples: BBQ with smoke!

Mouth Watering Cake

For services, I recommend that you post a pic with your team. Bring your tools if possible.

Also – SMILE!

People will trust you more, I promise. Just skip the ADD TO FAVORITES part.

For your Preferred Page Audience, just ask yourself. Who are the most likely customers to buy my product?

Look at the past, who has bought something from you? Are they old? Male? Female? Where do they live?

The next step is to add a cover photo.

What's great about cover photos is you can also use it as a promotion tool.

You can add event details or promotion mechanics.

Let's look at some cover photos that you can copy or model from. Boyce Avenue

Boyce Avenue isn't a business but it's still applicable. They're announcing the band tour on their cover photo.

BBQ Restaurant

They are not announcing any promo but they are showing their best products on the cover.

Remember, perception is everything.

If the product looks great on the cover, then it must be good.

Are you selling a book or consulting?

Then try this one.

Add some quotes and some motivational words. Make it simple and appealing to the eye.

Once you have your cover photo, go straight to the settings and edit the page moderation.

Here, you can add words that you don't want other people to see.

Let us say someone said "fuck or you suck, or your bbq suck" on your fan page, then that will destroy your credibility.

However, if you add these words in your moderation, then no other people could see it except you and the one who said it.

Make sure that you're typing the EXACT word that you want to block.

In this case, the word "BBQ" will not be block. Just the words - > "your bbq suck" "fuck you" "stupid" and "your place suck"

Click SAVE CHANGES and you're done.

NEVER EVER FORGET TO DO THIS STEP.

You'll save a lot of time and heartbreaks in the future just by doing this one little thing.

Chapter 2 — Content Creation

Your content creation is crucial to your long term success. You cannot just promote product after product.

You also have to give them some valuable information or some kind of entertainment in the process.

The goal of your content is to make them bond with you and make them trust you.

The more initial transaction you have with your customers, the easier it will be to sell them your products in the future.

Types of Content to Post

Text

This is the most basic for a post. It's still an effective way to communicate but the bad thing is that it is very forgettable.

When was the last time you read a long text post?

Pictures

Posting a picture is a very effective way to communicate with your audience.

You can also create TEXT in pictures so instead of just posting a text post, you'll just post a picture.

Here is an example of a text to picture post from the page "The Millionaire Fast Lane" (which is a book)

It has 1.4k likes

To apply this in your business, you can post something related to your market and ask for people's feedback.

Let's say you're a Restaurant owner. You can post something like this.

Or if you're selling your advertising services, then do something like this one: (I got this from the Ogilvy & Mather page)

Your content shouldn't just sell your products and services. It should stand for what you believe in or what you stand for.

Videos

Videos are also an effective way to talk to your customers. It takes a little bit more effort but if you have something interesting to say, then they will watch your video.

You can try these simple suggestions to get them to watch your video

- make it HD quality video

- Giveaway prizes

- give away discounts and in the video, explain what they need to do to get that discounts

- Hire celebrities. Don't worry, it doesn't have to be an award winning artist.

D – Memes and GIFS

Not all businesses can pull this off but if you are in some sort of entertainment business, then this can tremendously help you in the bonding process with your cus-tomers.

You can get your memes on Google images and your GIFS on GIPHY.Com

Chapter 3 — How to Gain More Followers & Promote Your Business

We are going to be growing our fan page and promote products at the same time.

We're going to sue the power of virality to do this. Here's how we would do it.

#1 – Friends, Family and Current Customers

If I am just starting out, what I would do is I will reach out to my friends, family and even current customers.

Email them or personally talk to them. You can also message them on Facebook to like your new business page.

If you can get 20-50 likes then that a pretty good starting point.

#2 – Fiverr

Another way to get Facebook fans is to promote your fan page by using Fiverr.

These are not highly targeted people but it can help you grow "likes" which can serve as social proof for your business. (If a lot of people are liking this page then this must be worth "liking" for)

#3 – Free Giveaways

One of the most effective ways to get more fans is to ran a giveaway for your product. Tell them that the giveaways would only be given to the people who will like and share the giveaway promo post.

You can also do a physical giveaway promo for your current customers.

For example. Post something like this on Facebook.

Attention Cake Lovers!

From 3pm-5pm tomorrow November 6, 2016

Everyone who'll buy our new chocolate burst cake will get another one for free! Like and Share this post because we will also choose one lucky winner who will get it for free!

(You can claim your prize on the store itself or we will deliver it to you NO CHARGE as long as you're in Nashville Area)

Here's another example for information marketers out there.

#3.1 The Simple Giveaway Funnel

Simply post something valuable on your feed and ask them to check it out. The content will be posted on your blog or website.

One of my favorite marketer is Ryan Deiss.

He's really smart and has very analytical mind. Here's a post he made recently.

If the image is a bit blurry, let me explain what he did.

He introduces an expert on a topic and tell why we should listen to this expert.

Then he told us what this expert is going to show us.

Lastly, he gave the benefit of reading and checking out whatever he is trying to share. Then he just give a link. That's it.

#4 Run a Contest

This is almost the same as a giveaway. The difference being is that only a few people will get the free product.

ALWAYS tell your audience that they will only be eligible to receive the product if they will LIKE and SHARE the content shared.

You can even give away products unrelated to yours but I would suggest that you start with your own.

One of the most famous products to give as a contest prize is an apple product.

#5 – Write A Short Kindle Book About Your Business

If you are selling courses about getting a job interview then you can write something about job interview FAQs, how to answer job interview calls etc.

If you are a Plumber then you can write something about, How to choose a plumber or 7 Ways To Unclog The Toilet.

It doesn't have to be hundreds of pages. A short 15- 25 pages book will do! Price them at ZERO (perma free) to get a many people as possible.

What I want you to do is at the beginning and the last page of the book, ask them to like your fan page to continue communicating with you or tell them that they can reach out on Facebook by messaging you through your fan page.

#6 – Connect Your FB page to your other social media accounts.

Once you connected your fb to your twitter, instagram etc. You can now focus on only one social platform when posting your content. Instead of posting one by one on each social media page, you just do it once and VOILA , you"re done. You'll be able to reach more people with less effort.

WARNING

If you do this, make sure that you'll still continue to communicate with customers and make sure that you'll still answer their questions.

Most businesses who connect their social media accounts start to forget to continue to use their other accounts.

How to connect your FB to other social medias.

The best way to do this is to use IFTT or If This Then That.

What IFTT does is to make this process so much easier than before. IFTT has frameworks called recipes.

What it dos is to automate the posting process of posting content to various social media sites.

Let's say you post a promotion on Facebook. If you use the recipe below, IFTT will automatically post that content on Evernote.

Another famous example is the " If Facebook, Then twitter" recipe.

You simply post on your content on FB and it'll automatically be tweeted on Twitter!

You can also post on other social networks instead on posting on Facebook first.

Here are some of the recipes that I used in the past.

Another awesome feature of IFTT is that it lets you schedule a post.

So if you're going on a vacation for 5 days then you can schedule your post and it'll automatically post content on your feed.

Isn't that awesome?

#7 – SEO Power

Another one of my best kept secret is SEO. Not a lot of business owners think of ranking their FB page on Google's Page 1.

I don't blame them; it seems complicated at first.

But in reality, it's really as simple as counting 1 2 3. Here's the easiest way to do this.

FIVERR.

If you haven't noticed yet, I really love Fiverr.

I can hire super cheap quality workers here.

What I would do first is to make a list of 3 keywords that I want to rank for in Google.

Say I'm a Delaware Plumber.

The keywords that I may want to rank for are the following:

Delaware Plumbing

Delaware Best Plumber

Best Plumber in Delaware

What I would do next is to get my FB page link.

You did this on chapter 1.

Hire Someone on Fiverr to send backlinks

What I would do next is to hire someone on Fiverr to send backlinks to my website.

I usually get 5 different backlinking services.

Give keywords and Link

The next step is to just give the keywords you want to rank for and the link to your fb page. They will do the rest for you.

Now, am I sure that I'm going to rank on page 1. Nope.

Some keywords have much more competition and sometimes, it takes a few weeks or months to see a movement of page ranking.

I learned to be much patient when it comes to SEO these days.

Additional tips for FB Fan Page SEO Domination

Optimize Title

If you can, put your keyword in your business page name. If not, make sure that you optimize your description properly.

Optimize Description

In your description area, include the following:

- your phone number

- your website

- your complete address

- your keywords (if you're trying to rank for

INTERNATIONAL SEO FIRM, then put it on the description) Example: (You can edit your description in the ABOUT page)

Chapter 4 — Facebook Ads for Beginners

A d Goal, Your Goal

The type of ad that you will create will depend on whatever is your goal.

There are so much ad types that it can be confusing at time. Thankfully, you don't really need to know or test all of them once you know your ad goal.

Some ad types may overlap with each other.

For example, say you're selling a Game of Thrones key-chain, then the best type of ad for you could be Clicks to Website or Website Conversions. It could also be Page Post Engagement if you want a lot of engagement between you and your potential customers first. Either one could be good, you just have to test it.

In general, here are the guidelines that I follow whenever I choose an ad type to use.

Note:

There are 3 categories for ad types.

Awareness, Consideration and Conversion.

You will see the AD TYPE NAME when you click on the options itself. For example,

BOOST YOUR POST

A Boost Your Post option is called PAGE POST ENGAGEMENT or PPE.

TYPES OF ADS

#1 – Clicks to Website

No question, the most used of them all.

It's easy to set up and pretty straight to the point.

CTW is perfect if you want to send them OUT of Facebook.

Maybe you want them to order or buy something from your website? Use it.

#2 – Website Conversions

Website conversion is best especially if you want to track your customer's actions.

You either want to track the following: CONTENT VIEW

ADD TO CART PURCHASE

This is best used for ecommerce stores.

#3 – Page Post Engagements

PPE is perfect if you don't have any fans yet.

If you want to build your fan base first, then PPE is highly recommended.

Also, make sure that you engage in other people's comments.

#4 – Page Likes

This one is also great for those who are just getting started.

If you have ZERO to 100 likes on your fan page, this is the best way to build that initial fans and create traction and trust for your business.

#5 – App Installs

Do you have an app that you want to promote? Then this is the best ad type to use.

#6 – App Engagement

Same thing ad #5, it's just a combination of app install + those who would like to talk about it on the comments section.

#7 – Offer Claims

Do you have some discounts or one time offers? Then this is the ad type to use!

#8 - Local Awareness

Great for local or small businesses.

If you want to target people from a specific city or zip code, then this one is perfect.

#9 – Event Responses

If you want to promote a special event, use this.

It could be your yearly 50% off, or free booze or whatever!

#10 – Product Catalog Promotion

Do you have some kind of product line up that you want to promote?

Then use this. It's almost like CTW except that you're promoting 3-5 products in just one ad.

#11 – Brand Awareness

You're a new business or you have a new product, service or place that you want to expose in the market?

In that case, this is the ad type to use.

#12 – Lead Generation

If you want to build a customer list or you want to get customer's information to contact later, use this.

#13 – Video Views

Want to rack up your video views for pennies on the dollar? You know what to do.

Depending on your purpose, choose just ONE AD TYPE to test for your first Facebook ad.

I don't want you to get overwhelm by this.

Also, whatever type of ad you chose, you're still going to follow the same guidelines for ad creation anyway.

So don't think about it too much!

If you're stuck, I recommend any of the following:

Click to Website Website Conversions

Page Post Engagements

I use any of these 3 95% of the time!

So let's go straight to the next chapter and let's start creating your first ad.

Chapter 5 — Setting Up Your First Ad & Market Targeting

Alright, it's time to create your first ad.

On the upper right side, click CREATE ADS.

You should have a fan page already before you create an ad) Choose the type of ad you want to create.

Choose a name.

I recommend "ProjectName – 1" Then click continue.

When it comes to targeting, you have to know who your audience is.

The key is understanding who are the people who are most likely to buy from you. Also, it would be great if you already have some past customers.

Who are they? How old? Men? Women?

You have to know this! It's your business we're talking about. Let's do this via an example.

Say that you're selling a course on How to Make Money for Home for Moms.

Then you have to ask yourself the questions I mentioned above. Now, my targeting would look like this:

For Interest targeting, I would look at possible demographics that may match my target market.

Besides the demographics, I can also target FAN PAGES related to work at home mom or work at home opportunities.

I only choose "INTERESTS" and NOT Employers & Job Titles.

For Potential Reach, I recommend that you have at least 1,000,000.

And then you EDIT PLACEMENT and you follow this set up below.

Always start with FEEDS only.

For the Daily Budget, I always start with $20.

Leave the optimization as it is.

And then rename your ad and click continue.

In the ad format, you can choose between 4 different formats.

For beginners, I recommend SINGLE IMAGE or SINGLE VIDEO. Again, this would depend on what your ad goal is.

Do you want to get more ad clicks? Do you want exposure? You can't have it all in just one ad.

Say that you chose IMAGE, here are the image size guidelines you can follow.

Your image should be HD or clean-looking.

It doesn't have to be perfect, it just has to stand out. Also, your image should only have 20% text on it.

Here's an example:

Once you have an image, input your website url next.

Then the headline and text.

On the next chapter, I'll teach you what and how to write your ad content, for now, just put anything here.

Once you're done, just click Review Order to see what your ad looks like and then click Place Order.

And you're done with the ad set up.

That may seem longer in theory but when you do it on your own, it actually only takes less than 10 minutes to do!

On the next chapter, we'll focus on how to create the ad content.

This is your ad content:

It is what the final ad looks like in action.

Chapter 6 — Ad Content & Ad Evaluation

This will be a really quick lesson but valuable nonetheless. Your ad content will always have 4 layers.

1 – The Headline 2 – The Text

3 – The Call to Action 4 – The Image

Let's use an example that I got from HUBSPOT.

Let's break this down one by one.

The Headline

The headline is "Get 3 Bottles for $19"

What is it that you are offering? Tell it on the headline!

For my Game of Thrones ad, it's "100% FREE GAME OF THRONES PENDANT"

It's straight to the point and it clearly said what I'm trying to offer.

The Text

The text is a little bit tricky, but in general, I'll just call out the target market and then explain what they are getting.

It's like a one sentence summary of your offer.

The Call to Action

The Call to Action depends on what you're trying to get from your potential customers.

Is it their email? Phone number? A purchase?

The Image

The Image is CRUCIAL!

You have to make sure that your image clearly shows the product you are promoting.

If it's a service, make sure that you have some kind of image that shows people talking to each other or doing the service itself.

Once you have some ad running, you have to test it for 3-5 days and see the results for yourself.

But how do you know whether to stop an ad, scale it or cut the budget?

HOW TO EVALUATE RESULTS

Here are things that may happen after 3-4 days of testing.

#1 – You get zero sales and only few clicks/comments/likes

STOP THE AD AND CHOOSE ANOTHER PRODUCT.

You need to change your product or service to offer…. or at least run it 3 more days with a different product angle.

#2 – You got a lot of clicks/comments/likes but not sales or any leads

Your product is either too expensive or the shipping is too expensive as well. Change it and make it a little bit cheaper.

For services, your offer probably sucks.

#3 - You got 1 or 2 sale and lots of comments/likes (Or you got a few leads for your business)

You have a great product and offer. Just continue running your ads and tweak your targeting by changing the age and gender of your target. You can see all these details on the ad manager.

#4 – You got more than 3 sales and lots comments/likes (You got lots of leads and your satisfy with your ad-spend: customer ratio)

Increase your ad budget by 100%. Keep running the ad as long as you are getting positive ROI.

Chapter 7 — Twitter Marketing for Beginners

Setting Up Your Profile

Register your account first on Twitter.com

Use your business name or brand name as your full name.

Then input your phone number and country, and then next, is one of the most important part.

Your Twitter handle.

Don't use any hyphens or complicated spellings. Try to make it short and easy to pronounce.

The test is if you're telling your Twitter to a friend, would she easily understand what you said and how to spell it?

For example,

The word UNLIMITEDSHIRTS is pretty easy to understand and spell.

This one is a good one.

However if you use: UNLIIIISHIIIRTS

Then this would be harder to spell and tell!

Try to be as short and straight forward as possible.

AVATAR or PROFILE PICTURE.

This is the first thing they will look at aside from your handle.

If possible, always show someone smiling in your profile picture.

An alternative could be the logo of your business. Examples:

Next is your cover photo.

If you have an ecommerce business, I recommend that you put pictures of your products. If you own a service type business, then just put your promos or the picture of your team in your cover photo.

Information Products from Eben Pagan.

Anyway, don't make this step complicated. Just use any decent photos you have that is related to your business if you can't think of anything to use.

Just don't leave it blank.

Use it instead of making it a waste of advertising space.

The next step is to edit your profile.

The Bio should give a one sentence info about who you are/what your business is all about.

Then put your location.

And then never forget to include your website url.

You can get some extra traffic just by simply putting your website url in that section.

Then click Save Changes.

You now have a proper set up finished.

Now, it's time to understand some terminologies that you may encounter and use to grow your Twitter marketing account.

Chapter 8 — Understanding Terminologies

To better understand how to market on Twitter, you gotta know first some terminologies that will help you use Twitter more effectively.

Here are they:

Hashtags

Hashtags are used to find words or tweets about a certain topic.

Examples of hashtags are - #Hereatsubway #enjoyingmyfood

If you want to promote a specific product or your business in general, you can put your product name on a hashtag.

Example – #SelectsNewIcecream , #yummyicrecream

Be warned though, too many hashtags can get annoying sometimes.

Retweet (RT)

You can use this function to share other people's tweets to your own followers.

Trending

From the word itself, it is something that is trending on twitter. It can be a word, a guy, whatever. This just means a lot of people are tweeting about that stuff.

Example - When Jon Snow died in Game Of Thrones #JonSnow trended worldwide.

Mention

If you want to give credit or tag someone on a tweet, you just have to mention their name... which is "@username" (whatever their username is)

Direct Message (DM)

If you want to message someone just like on Facebook, you can message them through twitter's Direct Message.

Tweets

This is basically Twitter's version of a Post.

Follower/s

Someone who is subscribe in your business through twitter

Chapter 9 — Building Your Followers

Now that we've got everything set up properly, it's time to find some followers or customers.

Here are some steps to take to get followers on twitter.

Tweet some useful and related stuff

Make some value tweets to your community, people will eventually find these tweets through hashtags and your tweets nature.

Ex. Let's say your niche is Search Engine Optimization

Then give them an article about SEO. (Sample tweet below)

Keep giving value tweets and you'll eventually get some followers in your topic.

In your tweet, You can also ask them to follow you.

Make a habit of spend at least 20-30 minutes a day on twitter, just continue to provide value. Link them to your own website if you have some content already.

Search for hashtags and related tweets.

To get more followers, search for related tweets in your niche and follow the people who are tweeting these tweets.

To get them to follow you, give them a good reason to follow you.

Tweet them about something that can help them

In the picture above, we can see that Ryan Rodriguez is posting about seo articles.

We can simply tweet Ryan and give him possibly more information. or we can thank him for the article and ask for a follow back.

Example:

Click the reply button and thank Ryan for his article. Just repeat the process and build your followers.

Solve their problems

Find someone who may need your help

You can find them by searching what I call "HELP TERMS"

If you're a plumber in Utah then try to search " plumbers in New York" "Help I need a plumber New York upstate area"

Just search something someone would type when they are needing one's help for something.

Steal Them

This is my favorite way to find customers. What do we do?

We steal them! Legally.

We just search for competition and look at their followers.

When I search "plumbers Utah", there's a ton of companies tweeting about their business.

Just click their name and go to their profile. Click FOL-LOWERS.

Then manually follow these people, it is probably worth your time to follow these guys because they are buyers who are already following a service they'd probably use.

Click "follow" to be their follower.

Then tweet them and give them some value instead of selling.

Or give them special offers that you know you're the only one who could offer.

The Power of Retweeting

You can retweet people's tweets especially if you think these tweets are useful or atleast related to your niche.

Say someone is ranting about how his roof is always leaking,

Retweet it.

Click the circling arrow button to re-tweet.

Alternative to re-tweet or replying.

If you want too, you can also send private messages on twitter; they call it "direct message" or DM for short.

To do this, just click the name and go to his /her profile.

Click MESSAGE

Note: Some people can't be DM depending on their settings.

There are thousand more ways to gain followers through twitter but these are the basic beginner's stuff.

Heck, some beginners don't even use some of these tactics.

The most important thing to do is to be consistent in always providing solutions to your customers.

If you're sharing good stuff out there, then good karma will come back to you.

Chapter 10 — Selling on Twitter

Selling on Twitter requires a strategy and not just some random tweets.

Also, the worst thing that you can do is to just tweet some link all the time.

You just can't SELL SELL SELL.

You have to GIVE GIVE GIVE.... And then you sell. Here's a strategy that you can follow.

This is not a set in the stone strategy. You can change it if you want too. It's up to you.

But this is what I do and what I teach my students to do.

I call it the Twitter Warfare Strategy (TWS)

In TWS, the strategy requires you to post at least 1 tweet every 3 hours. You can do this by using automation tools for Twitter posting (which I'll give you a list of on chapter 5).

The sequence of tweets works like this.

Information

On your first tweet, give them some kind of related information on your topic. It can be a link to an article or a simple tweet related to your topic/business.

Giphy

The next tweet is to get some GIF files related to your business.

For example, say you're selling SEO SERVICES.

You can find a funny GIF on GIPHY.COM and tweet something like this:

"When they say that SEO is dead..."

Quotes

Your quotes could be text or images. Again, it must be something related to your business.

Have a restaurant? Tweet something like this.

Quotes

(follow instructions on #3)

Current Events

You can also tweet something that is related to some current events.

Make sure that you make your stand on some issues but don't be in it too much. You don't want people tweeting you about Donald Trump.

Quotes

(follow instructions on #3)

Information

Give them an article or blogpost that can help them solve whatever their problem is.

Sell

This is the time to sell!

Tweet them a link or a discount code for your product. Don't try to hard-sell them on your products.

Remember, you have a lot of opportunity to do this, but you have to build that trust in your relationship first.

Bring as much value and entertainment and they will love you long term!

Chapter 11 — Automating Your Twitter Feed

Automating on Twitter is one of the best ways to make your life so much easier.

You have to make sure though that you're not just tweeting some random stuff that has nothing to do with your customers.

These tools are for automation but that doesn't necessarily mean that you won't care anymore.

Check it out and always make sure that your tweets are still connecting to your audience.

Here are some tools to use if you want to automate the process.

HootSuite

It allows you to schedule tweets and get RSS feeds from these tweets.

SocialOomph

It allows you to schedule tweets, send automatic direct messages, automatically follow your followers and also create bulk tweets.

Twaitter

Can be used for automatic tweets and translating tweets.

Chapter 12 — Instagram Marketing for Local Business

Your Magic Powers

Every small business out there has to have some kind of magic powers that their 100 loyal customers love.

Your magic power is basically one thing your business is the best at.

"But dude, my business caters to everyone and we're the best at everything we do!"

Stop right there. That's not true at all.

If you want to compete, then you gotta have a specialty for your business. This doesn't mean that the other parts of your business is bad.

Nope. This only means that you're really really great at this one thing. For example:

Say you're a "BBQ Guy"

You own a BBQ restaurant and you have a menu like: Texas BBQ

Mexican BBQ

Whatever kind of BBQ Other Menus

You don't have to be the TEXAS BBQ GUY or the MEXICAN BBQ guy, you can be the BBQ GUY, but at the same time, you must have really good sub-menus other than your BBQ.

However, you can also specialize as the MEXICAN BBQ GUY. No one's stopping you from doing this.

The key is to know what you're good at and focus at it.

Once you have your magic powers, you can start focusing your marketing efforts with it in mind.

You don't have to promote that specific products every time, but it will be the cornerstone of your brand.

For example:

KFC

They have lots of other products but their main draw is their fried chicken.

Some Plumber Here in my Town

If you only have one product, then you have to make it unique. A plumber in my town has a 30 for 1 deal.

He'll be there in 30 minutes and he'll fix it in an hour.

Obviously, he knows whether he can fix it or not in time even before he agrees with the deal.

Cinnabon

Cinnabon's main product is cinnamon rolls. How about you?

What is your magic power?

The Power of Branding

A strong brand separates you from your competition. Build a strong brand and you'll never go hungry again.

Your customers will automatically come to you and your business will always be their first choice.

So how do you build a brand that people like and people will connect with?

The answer is through STORIES.

Stories are powerful way to persuade and connect with your customers.

And the best thing about Instagram is you can tell these stories via Images and Videos!

How to apply this in your business?

You can tell your story through pictures

Pictures have the ability to convey emotion and stories.

Post a picture of your business when you were just starting out and tell them how grateful you are to your customers, tell them that you were able to do all of these because of them.

A history wall

I remember when I was eating at my local KFC. I saw these "history wall" and I was able to feel that sense of connection. I don't know if it's just me or not. But the point is, it may help your build a brand for your business.

Share customer testimonials

Part of your story is how you make your customers happy. Take a picture of them while they are on your business establishment and put a quote of their testimonial on the picture.

They are not telling a story but a picture of them on your establishment does convey a story of "Hey, my customers love my business and they go here every time they need my service"

Videos

You can also shoot 30-60 second testimonials and share them on Instagram.

Exercise/Action Steps:

1. Take a picture of your current customers while they are at your business

2. Always ask for feedback and testimonials

3. Write your own story. Answer these questions to formulate your own Home town boy makes good

story.

Plus, answer these additional questions.

1. Why did I start the business aside from monetary reasons?

2. Why do I love my business?

3. What are the things I have to go through before making this business a success?

4. What can I consider the small failures and small wins for my business?

5. Write your biggest breakthrough. A certain experience or happening when it all changes for your business.

Chapter 13 — How to Create Powerful Posts

In this chapter, you'll learn the importance of having a systematic way of creating content.

I am not gonna teach you how to edit images, you can practice that in your own time and leisure.

But I will recommend some tools for editing that you can use for free or for as cheap as possible.

Here are the best editing tools to use for Instagram.

You have to have some kind of mobile device or tablet/iPad to use these applications.

A – Instagram B – Fotor

C – Qwik

D – VSCO Cam

E – Lensical

F – PicLab HD

G – Photoristic HD H – Handy Photo

I – Path On

J – Camera +

K – Photoshop Express

You don't have to have all of them.

In fact, just find one (or two) that you're comfortable with and just use it.

HOW TO CREATE A POST

Every image post will have 3 important parts.

The Image

For the image, you have to be clear of what you're trying to achieve.

Are you trying to motivate them? Are you trying to show them your product? Are you giving them a discount? Are you trying to engage them in a conversation?

Before you post an image, always be clear of your intentions.

Trying to shoe social proof + products?

Don't just post anything you can think of.

Try to be strategic in your posts and always have a goal for that one post.

Note:

Another thing you have to be weary of is consistency. Don't use a lot of different filters or style in your photos.

If you use black and white, then don't make it a random post. Use it every 6 posts. Make it consistent.

Too many filters will make your Instagram look awful. This one is actually pretty great:

This one, not so much. It feels random.

The Description

For the description, it should match your goal and your image.

If you have a post showing your bakery's cinnamon, then post something related to that image.

For example:

They say that cinnamon is good for the heart. We have no clue if it's true but Valentine's day is coming and couples are already flocking the store looking for our awesome couple deals!

Make it fun and make it sound original.

You can't be boring and expect people to generate conversation with you.

In some way, you have to be a little bit controversial sometimes.

Here's an example of what you shouldn't do or even if you do this, make sure that you don't do it a lot!

"Come to our store and buy our new couple's cinnamon rolls!" It's just blatant sales pitch and that's not too fun for most people. Here are some awesome descriptions:

A coffee shop aiming to get young customers. If you're target market is old people, then this description probably won't work.

Another example of a simple but awesome post.

The Hashtag

The next part of having a powerful post is the hashtag. The hashtag is basically a way to:

A – Make other people discover you

B – To show what your photo is all about

With this in mind, every post that you have should AL-WAYS satisfy these two guidelines.

When you're thinking of hashtags to use, try looking for other businesses related to yours and just copy what they're doing.

Are you selling Texas BBQ?

Then search for Texas BBQ and then see what others are using.

I recommend that you have at least 7-10 hashtags per post. Every hashtag is an opportunity to reach more people but too much may be too annoying for the eyes.

So search for your main term and...

Look for other hashtags related to your main hashtag.

As long as it is highly related to your post, you can also use these terms and get more customers!

Open some posts made by other pages and look at what hashtags they are using.

Then steal it! It's not like its illegal or something.

Now that you know the anatomy of a powerful post, it's time to increase your followers!

Chapter 14 — How to Get More Instagram Followers

There's a lot of little things you can do to increase your follower count. Before you do these tricks, make sure that you understand first

how to create a powerful post. If you're Instagram is boring, then no one will follow you.

Got it?

Ok, let's start.

Here are my top 7 ways to increase your Instagram followers.

Images

I can't stress this enough.

If your images suck, then you won't grow your fan page. Practice editing images and make them pretty.

Instagram is a billion-dollar photo app for a reason!

People love images and they expect higher quality than your bathroom selfie.

Instagram Celebrities

In every niche, there are people you can contact to promote your product or service.

Got a hip new restaurant?

Then go search for people who are always posting their "food travels", contact them and make them try your product for free.

If you contact 10 people and each of them have 2,000 followers, then you can easily get your money's worth!

You just have to make sure that this guy/gal have a good time and let them know that you appreciate him/her for trying the product.

If you both like each other enough, you can struck a deal with them and they will promote your product every once in a while.

This is more powerful than just promoting the product on your own. If other people are seeing that you're getting promoted by someone they like and respect, then they are more likely to be your follower and customer.

Hashtags

We've discussed this already but it's worth repeating.

Always try as many hashtags as possible and track your followers counts. Does a certain group of hashtags somehow increase your likes and comments? Then keep using it!

Discount code

Having promos can also increase not only your followers but your actual sales!

For example: "Show this post in our store and you'll automatically get a 5% discount code! Bring a friend and you'll get 10% discount!"

Instagram Videos

Variety is important, that's why you also have to have some videos every once in a while.

Make it short and funny if possible.

It can also be customer testimonials or customers holding the products themselves.

Follow your likers

Not all of your post likers will follow your account.

Just follow as many as you can, some of them will actually follow you back because… I don't know. That's just how the power of reciprocity works.

Holidays

Use hashtags related to an upcoming holiday. You'll get a lot of new followers by doing this one thing alone.

#MerryChristmas #HappyJuly4th #LaborDay

Chapter 15 — Promotion Strategy

So you now know how to create content and how to get followers. So how do you actually make money from your followers without being salesy and annoying?

One word: STRATEGY

You can't just ask your followers to BUY BUY AND BUY.

You have to give them amazing content before you ask something from them.

Here is the ration that is safe to follow. 9:1

Nine is to one.

For every 9 post that you'll do, one is a blatant sales pitch. This badly Photoshop image is my version of your profile.

All blue box (that's a box!) contains CONTENT ONLY without you asking for a sale or without you asking for them to buy anything from you.

I recommend that you do 2-3 post per day so you'll have 3 days of content and then 1 day (1 post) of promotion.

After your 9 content post, you can create a post asking them to buy from you or visit your store or to grab a discount code.

Be patient in your promotion strategy. This method of promotion is for long term gains.

Once you did you promotion, just repeat the process over and over again.

When it comes to your promotion post, you can do any of the following:

The Discount Method

Here, you'll offer a discount code for your products or services. This is effective only if you don't do it a lot. So don't give discounts every week. Give these discounts a time limit and make them use it immediately.

The Like and Comment

This is a viral promotion method. The more people who like and comment your post, the more Instagram is likely to give you a top spot for the hashtags you are using.

So you'll get the TOP POST spot.

The Event Method

The event method is where you'll announce a special event and ask them to physical attend it.

Always have some kind of special deal in these events. You can't just throw "special events" and then do the normal operation.

The Try This Specific Product Method

This is the most blatant (but still effective) way to sell your product. Just ask them to try or buy it.

You can make this a little bit of fun though.

By adding a well-crafted description, you can make the promotion sound like a content instead of a promo post.

For example:

New Coffee Flavor Alert!

Have a taste of our new coffee and bond with our awesome and beautiful baristas!

Plus, meet some new cool friends who loves coffee as much as you do!

So start doing this content-promotion strategy and start getting new and loyal customers for your business today.

Milton Keynes UK
Ingram Content Group UK Ltd.
UKHW020637010823
426141UK00015B/667

9 789994 914494

NASHARITES

INTERCESSORS FOR REVIVAL & THE RETURN
OF THE LORD

COREY RUSSELL

NASHARITE PUBLISHING

Nasharite Publishing
6350 S. Patsburg Court
Aurora, CO 80016

ISBN: 978-1-7369070-4-7 (paperback)
ISBN: 978-1-7369070-5-4 (e-book)

This book is dedicated to our son, Josiah Nash Russell,
his story, and the Nasharites, who are believing God for
revival in their families, churches, and nations.

CONTENTS

I have set watchmen on your walls, O Jerusalem; they shall never hold their peace day or night. You who make mention of the LORD, do not keep silent, and give Him no rest till He establishes and till He makes Jerusalem a praise in the earth.

THE PROPHET ISAIAH

AN ARMY OF INTERCESSORS

I believe the Church is in the middle of the greatest reformation the world has ever seen. On both a local and global level, Sunday-only Christianity is over. 2020 brought that to a stop. The Church has since entered a new season, where the ministry of prayer is moving from the back to the front room and where the Lord is marking a generation with the spirit of prayer for revival.

More specifically, God is raising up men and women in this generation who are intercessors and forerunners of revival. I call them *Nasharites*.

Named after Daniel Nash, a minister who partnered in prayer with Charles G. Finney during the Second Great Awakening in the early 1800s,

the Nasharites of our day, like their predecessor, storm the gates of hell in spiritual warfare, decreeing to the devil and his cohorts, "No more taking any of our generation captive, not on our watch!" And they cry out to God in travail, "Lord, rend the heavens and come down! Pour out Your Spirit upon all flesh."

With foreheads like flint, this army of intercessors gives themselves to prayer until God breaks through in His Church and in the earth—until He comes! These hidden prayer warriors have an understanding of their identity as sons and daughters of God, convinced that He hears them and answers their prayers. They possess a breaker anointing on their lives for the move of God in their homes, families, churches, towns, cities, and nations. Just like the eponymous Father Nash, the Nasharites are "mighty in prayer."

THE NASH STORY

Daniel Nash was a pastor in New York in the early 1800s. His path first crossed that of the great nineteenth-century revivalist, Charles G. Finney, on December 30, 1823. In his memoirs,

Finney wrote about this meeting for his ministry license:

> At this meeting of the presbytery I first saw Rev. Daniel Nash, who is generally known as "Father Nash." He was a member of the presbytery. A large congregation was assembled to hear my examination. I got in a little late, and saw a man standing in the pulpit speaking to the people, as I supposed. He looked at me as I came in; and was looking at others as they passed up the aisles. As soon as I reached my seat and listened, I realized that he was praying.[1]

Finney was none too impressed at that time by Nash. In fact, he thought Nash appeared "very cold and backslidden" because of the manner in which he prayed, eyes open and looking around the room.[2] It was after Nash's return home from this meeting, according to Finney, that Nash "was confined to his room with his eyes, and was almost entirely blind for about six months."[3] Writing about this long after Nash's death, Finney recounted in a letter dated July 7, 1875:

During this period, as he afterwards informed me, he gave himself to much prayer, had a great searching and overhauling spiritual life, and, before he could see enough to be abroad was powerfully baptized with the Holy Ghost. Soon after this he came to me in the midst of a powerful revival of religion at Evans Mills in the northern part of Jefferson County, N. Y. I could see that he had been made over, and was quite another man. He was full of the Holy Ghost. He had the strongest faith and was the mightiest man in prayer that I had ever met.[4]

Within the letter, Finney also noted the places where Nash had partnered with him in prayer:

Afterwards, he labored with me in revivals in Gouverneur and Dekalb in the southern part of St. Lawrence County. In the midst of the great revival in Rome, Oneida Co., he had labored in prayer and conversation with great effect. He followed on to Utica, and afterwards in Troy and New Lebanon east of the Hudson River. He was a most wonderful man in prayer, one of the most earnest, and devout, spiritually-minded, heavenly-minded men I ever saw.[5]

Finney and Nash parted for a season, Finney ministering in Pennsylvania and Delaware while Nash labored in Central and Northern New York.[6] But when Finney went to Rochester, New York, in 1830, Nash showed up and began praying with fellow prayer partner, Abel Clary. Through prayer with others like Clary, Nash would break up the fallow ground in the hearts of hard characters in the towns and cities they visited.

For a seven-year period from their first meeting, Finney and Nash worked together on many occasions in Upstate and Western New York. Nash would pray—at times forerunning the revival, even arriving a few weeks before meetings to begin interceding—and Finney would preach. They began to connect over this understanding that intercession wins the battles in the heavenlies, and it plows the ground so that the Word of God can come in great power, transforming the coldest and most indifferent souls.

Finney didn't need Nash's preaching, but he said he needed Nash's praying. Often hidden away in a room somewhere nearby, Nash plowed in prayer the soil of the hearts of men and women, and then Finney sowed precious seed on that

fertile soil that produced lasting fruit. As Evangelist J. Gilchrist Lawson noted,

> It was found by research that over eighty-five in every hundred persons professing conversion to Christ in Finney's meetings remained true to God, whereas seventy per cent of those professing conversion in the meetings of even so great an evangelist as Moody afterwards became backsliders.[7]

The power of God that flowed through Finney's revival campaigns is unparalleled. The revival is often credited, "directly . . . or indirectly . . . with conversions of around 500,000 people."[8] Eighty-five percent of the converts stood the test of time, which means they stayed faithful to Jesus for decades and even to the end of their days. That's amazing!

Finney and Nash understood the principles of intercession, evangelism, and revival. I believe they also discovered a profound secret: *Sons and daughters of God have authority in prayer to ignite revival.* In fact, not only does their prayer forerun revival, causing the initial sparks to fly, but it continues to fan the flames so that revival fire keeps spreading.

As one source commented regarding the Rochester (New York) Revival in 1830–1831,

> [Finney's] daily preaching and revival services moved listeners and led to public conversions, often of leading members of the community. Women and families helped spread the news of the revival through home visits and prayer groups. Due to the ecumenical nature of the revival, many Protestants from multiple denominations traveled up to 100 miles to hear him preach.
>
> This event served as the inspiration for several other revivals that spread across the Northeast and New England during the Second Great Awakening. Finney's preaching style served as a blueprint for future revivalists throughout the 19th century and into the 20th century.[9]

In this hour, I believe God is revealing anew the secret of our authority in prayer, and He is calling His Church to intercession for the spreading of the gospel and the great end-time ingathering of souls. God wants His Church to labor in prayer, like Nash, for breakthrough in the hearts of people so that the Word can be sown, having great and life-changing impact. And not just in

one or two people, I might add, but in the lives of many the world over! True revival sweeps over towns, cities, and nations.

So, that was an abbreviated recounting of the historical story of the "Prevailing Prince of Prayer," Daniel Nash.[10] Dying in 1831, his gravestone in Upstate New York marks this man's life with these words, "Daniel Nash. Co-laborer with Finney. Mighty in prayer." These last three words of Nash's epithet marked my life in a powerful and unexpected way. And I believe God is calling us all to take part in forerunning revival in the earth—He's wanting us to become mighty in prayer.

WHO ARE THE NASHARITES?

Put simply, the Nasharites are people upon whom rests a spirit of prayer. I've heard it said before that the spirit of prayer resting on someone is the rarest anointing on earth. I believe that's true; however, this anointing is going to become more prevalent as many of us respond to the call to pray in these last days for the nations and the great harvest of souls.

During the Finney revival, it's interesting to note that they frequently mentioned the spirit of prayer and its effect upon both the individual praying and on the person being prayed for. Writing of seeing Nash praying, Finney said,

> Those that knew him, during the period of which I speak will never forget his prayers, and the unutterable groanings with which he was exercised by the Holy Spirit. The manifest and instantaneous answer to some of his prayers was so startling as to arrest the attention of everybody about him. . . .
>
> . . . . But soon he would come down and take the load of unconverted sinners upon [his] heart, and such agonizing, prevailing prayers I [have] never heard [from] any other man. Many times in meetings his soul became so full of anguish that he could not remain and keep silent. He would hastily and as slyly as possible retire from the meeting, seek a place where he could pour out his soul to God, and for hours would continue to wrestle and agonize, and groan his soul out to God, till his strength was completely exhausted. The spirit of prayer that was upon him was quite a stumbling-block to professors of religion, who had never known

the Holy Ghost as the Spirit that maketh intercession for the saints according to the will of
God with groanings that cannot be uttered. I
should here say, that very much of this type of
prayer prevailed in the revivals through central
and northern New York at that time. Many
laymen and women were exercised in a similar
manner, and sometimes would [stay] all night
in their closets with unutterable groanings for
the salvation of sinners.[11]

This is the same spirit of prayer that is gripping
the hearts of the Nasharites and, hopefully,
laying hold of our hearts today. It produces in us
deep weeping, groaning, and travail. As we will
see in the following pages, it brings us into beautiful union with the heart of God.

The spirit of prayer also brings with it a great
confidence in our beloved identity as sons and
daughters of God. As a result, when we move
into intercession for someone or for breakthrough in general, we are convinced the Lord
hears our prayers and will answer them. Then
when we begin to pray like the early church
prayed in Acts 4:24–29, we will receive an Acts
4:31 result:

> And when they had prayed, the place where they were assembled together was shaken; and they were all filled with the Holy Spirit, and they spoke the word of God with boldness.

In the pages that follow, we will unlock the DNA of the Nasharites—the hidden intercessors for revival. This army of Nasharites are people who love the Word of God, are intimate with the Father, have a revelation of intercession, and have a passion for revival.

Beloved, I believe that God wants to mark you with the spirit of prayer. He wants you to become a part of what I'm trusting Him for, which is an army of 100 million Nasharite intercessors who will keep watching and praying until Jesus receives "the nations for" His inheritance "and the ends of the earth" for His possession (Ps 2:8).

---

1. Charles G. Finney, *The Memoirs of Reverend Charles G. Finney,* (New York: A. S. Barnes & Company, 1876).
2. Finney, *The Memoirs of Reverend Charles G. Finney.*
3. P. C. Headley, *Evangelists in the Church: From Philip A. D. 35, to Moody and Sankey, A. D. 1875,* (Boston: Henry Hoyts, 1875), 71.
4. Headley, *Evangelists in the Church,* 71.
5. Headley, *Evangelists in the Church,* 71.

6. Headley, *Evangelists in the Church*, 71.

7. J. Gilchrist Lawson, *Deeper Experiences of Famous Christians Gleaned from Their Biographies, Autobiographies and Writings*, (Anderson, IN: The Warner Press, 1911), 243.

8. *Christianity Today*, "Christian History/Charles Grandison Finney: Did You Know?" Accessed October 10, 2023, https://www.christianitytoday.com/history/issues/issue-20/charles-grandison-finney-did-you-know.html/.

9. This information comes from a slide on a timeline titled, "Prominent Religious Events and People," The Association of Religion Data Archives, accessed October 23, 2023, https://www.thearda.com/us-religion/history/timelines/interactive-display?tid=1/.

10. "Prevailing Prince of Prayer" is part of a title of a book about Daniel Nash. J. Paul Reno, *Daniel Nash: Prevailing Prince of Prayer*, (Skyland, NC: Revival Literature, 1989).

11. Headley, *Evangelists in the Church*, 71.

A PERSONAL STORY & A BIBLICAL REALITY

T hough I didn't understand it initially, I soon realized through a series of events in my life that God was at work connecting the personal story of Nash and that of my own with a biblical reality. Often, the way I see this connection is like that of a small tributary which feeds into a larger river and finally flows into the sea of what God is going to do before He returns to the earth. It's typically how God connects all of our stories to His greater narrative.

MY FAMILY'S STORY

My wife, Dana, and I were born again during an incredible season of revival in high school. Since

then, we have read stories on historical awakenings and revivals. I've consumed them, in fact. Of course, one of the stories that greatly impacted us was that of Father Nash. It gripped Dana and me so much that we named our son after Daniel Nash.

After having received several prophecies that a son was coming, and after having been blessed with three beautiful daughters, the Lord gave us our boy, Josiah Nash Russell, in 2012. We didn't call him by his first name, however. We chose to call him Nash. Dana and I were delighted with our son, and the girls were happy to have a little brother. It was a beautiful time.

In March of 2013, something happened that rocked our family. Dana took Nash, nine-and-a-half months old at the time, and our girls to visit family in Arkansas. I couldn't be with them as I was in London, England, ministering. Then on March 16, 2013, Dana laid Nash down for a nap, but Nash never woke up. A horrible virus attacked his body, and he passed away in his sleep.

Our Nash's passing led our family into the darkest and most turbulent season of our lives. The truth is the past decade was gut-wrenching.

We asked all the questions that you ask after going through an experience like that. Grasping to understand what happened and why it happened, we were in the middle of the storm of grief and were overwhelmed, yet somehow I kept leaning into God, and He gave me a vision that shifted everything. It was the vision of the Nasharite army. It was then that I realized God was connecting our personal story to a biblical reality, to what God is going to do globally in the earth at the end of the age before He returns.

THE STORM & PSALM 2

In January 2014, still in the throes of great grief, I was in Mexico when the Holy Spirit said to me, "Corey, I want to give you the revelation of intercession." And He led me to Psalm 2. For the rest of 2014 and 2015, I lived in that chapter, as well as in Psalm 1. And I began asking God for my inheritance. I think I preached out of Psalm 2 at least 70 times in those two years.

The Holy Spirit used Psalm 2 to instruct me about the things that will take place on the earth before the Lord returns. For example, we will see the nations in a global unity, where kings, judges, and other players conspire against the Father and

the Son. And the aim of Satan's end-time plan is to overthrow Jesus' inheritance. This is the devil's major push—to steal the Father's inheritance for His Son.

But I also began to see Psalm 2, not only in the global end-time drama, but on a personal level regarding my family. Psalm 2 can be seen as a four-part drama. The first three verses speak of the chaos, confusion, and craziness of the time. Verses 4–6 depict the Father's perspective of the first three verses. And what we have is David asking, "Why is the Father laughing?"

Here is what I heard the Lord say to me on a personal level about the first two parts of Psalm 2: "Corey, I want you to come out of the chaos, confusion, and craziness, asking why. And I want to teach you how to ascend—how to get filled with divine confidence that no one is going to overthrow what I've promised you. I need you to come out of the swirl of what you see, taste, touch, and hear." In other words, He wanted me to gain a higher perspective and not bow down to my circumstances.

What the Lord taught me next was about coming up to Him who sits in the heavens and taking my seat "in the heavenly places" (Eph 2:6). It's there

that I can see Him laughing. The devil wanted to drag me down to the first heavens, where I would get caught up in the anxiety, the fear, and the anger that's there. But God wanted me to ascend in prayer to the third heaven where I was seated with Him, far above every principality, power, ruler, and dominion. He wanted me to pray from that place.

I must confess that it was awkward for me. It was difficult at first. I would say, "God, teach me how to ascend in the middle of feeling all alone, of feeling like I don't know how to navigate this." And that's when I moved into the third part of Psalm 2. Verses 7–9 changed my life!

In the third part of the psalm, in the midst of all the chaos that's raging and the Father laughing, Jesus entered the storyline. In Psalm 2:7–9, David overheard the following conversation between the Father and the Son:

> I will declare the decree: the LORD has said to Me, "You are My Son, today I have begotten You. Ask of Me, and I will give You the nations for Your inheritance, and the ends of the earth for Your possession. You shall break them with

a rod of iron; You shall dash them to pieces like
a potter's vessel."

This was where it all changed for me. *I saw what
Jesus was doing in the text. He was making eye contact
with the Father.* Instead of responding to the
chaos, He declared back to the Father what the
Father had spoken to Him. Here was my entry
into the ground level of spiritual warfare,
whereby God taught me how to fight when
things were the most chaotic and confusing. I
think it's very interesting that Father Nash, the
historical intercessor, was birthed into the spirit
of prayer through a hardship—through the six-
month loss of his sight. Through a very difficult
circumstance, Nash learned how to connect with
God in prayer. And that's what the Lord taught
me in the darkest days of my life.

Jesus wasn't screaming at the chaos or the
nations in Psalm 2. He wasn't trying to shout it
all down. No, He was looking at Abba Father,
declaring to His Father what the Father had
spoken over Him. And that became my prayer
assignment for the better part of a year-and-a-
half. The Father told me, "Corey, don't look at
that. Look at Me. Don't respond to that. Respond
to Me. Don't let those words dictate to you or

define you. Don't let the words you are hearing around you move you. But let My words safe-guard you in the middle of this season. And this is the first thing you need to hear from Me: *Corey, you are My son.*"

Surprisingly, God used Psalm 2 to heal my heart and give me a heavenly perspective. That chapter instructed me on what to believe for in the wake of the greatest loss of my life. It showed me that *the first revelation critical for intercessors, for Nasharites, is their beloved identity in Christ.* Being a daughter or son of the Father, being embraced and enjoyed by Him, means coming out of living in the front yard of Christianity. So many of us believers act like orphans living in the front yard, screaming in front of the house, while the Holy Spirit is inviting us all to come into the house. It's the Father's house—the house of prayer.[1] It's the only safe place for the days we are moving into. We need a Church living in the house instead of screaming in the front yard.

We need to be confident sons and daughters rooted in our beloved identity, having the revela-tion of the Father's affection and enjoyment of us. *We need to understand as well that the greatest places of warfare in our lives are our greatest places of*

inheritance. That's the other thing I learned from my family's storm and Psalm 2. The Father said to Jesus, "Ask Me for them, for the nations that are raging, and I'll make them Your inheritance."

THE DREAM

Then in 2015, after years of asking God for my inheritance, a friend named Jeremiah Johnson sent me a dream he had concerning me. He wasn't aware of what all had transpired in my life. He wrote me in May and said, "Corey, I had a powerful dream last night. I'm just gripped. I've been up all night with it. I can't shake it. I had a dream that the Church was under siege. It was like old medieval times, and everyone ran into the square. And as we realized that the cultural wars were increasing, we didn't know how to pray in these days." The next thing Jeremiah saw in the dream was my good friend, Allen Hood, and I walking into the scene, smiling. And we repeated a line twice to Jeremiah and those gathered in the dream, "These are the days we've been waiting on. These are the days we've been waiting on."

Jeremiah continued to explain what happened next, "I began to prophesy over you, 'Corey, for

every one voice of awakening, I'm going to raise up seven voices of intercession. I've given Lou Engle the Nazarites, but I'm about to raise up the Nasharites. And the Nasharites will be the hidden army of intercessors. They won't be known in the eyes of men, but they're going to be famous in heaven. I'm going to hear their prayers, and I'm going to hear their cries, and I'm going to send revival in their day."

That was an incredible affirmation of what God had been speaking to me about the Nasharite army of intercessors. I was very grateful to the Lord for giving my friend that dream. So, I went to call Jeremiah after I read his email, only just before I did, a number came out of my spirit, and I found myself saying, "God, give me 100 million Nasharites. Give me 100 million Nasharites— that's what I want as my inheritance. I want 100 million of them across the earth." I made a covenant with God in that moment and then said, "I'll let You do the accounting, but I'm going to proclaim this until I see You."

And over the last several years, I've been proclaiming this message. And, friend, I believe it is time. We are beginning to see the formation of a Nasharite army, which is an intercessory

army of people from every walk of life and every generation, all over the world, who are gripped with one resounding revelation: *God hears my prayers, and God's going to send revival in my home, in my church, in my city, and in my nation.*

I witnessed that very thing—God bringing healing and revival into my home. He not only healed me, but I watched as the Lord touched my girls and my wife, bringing healing to them over the loss of Nash. I watched the Lord lay hold of Dana in 2021, and she began to see what I was seeing. She began to emerge from the season of mourning and see the army of intercessors. And as soon as she came into that place of under-standing with me, I further understood what it was that God was doing in bringing the greatest reformation to the Church the earth has ever seen. Together, we began to burn, wanting to see change and revival come to individuals, families, towns, cities, and nations. And our cry became, "Let us be a part of seeing this 100-million Nasharite army of intercessors arise in the earth —for the outpouring of the Spirit, the return of the Lord, and the salvation of Israel."

I believe God gave us a tributary into a global storyline. He showed Dana and me—by what He

did in our family—that *the Holy Spirit is marking simple, everyday people like us and is releasing a revelation of the profound glory of intercession.* It's the power of weak words before the throne. It's the cry of Habakkuk's prayer, "O LORD, revive Your work in the midst of the years! In the midst of the years make it known; in wrath remember mercy" (3:2).

ACTS 4 & PSALM 2

Another portion of Scripture that came alive to me during this time was Acts 4, specifically where the early church quoted Psalm 2 in prayer. But Acts 4 opens with Peter and John being arrested. In Acts 3, we're told that Peter and John healed the lame man at the Beautiful Gate, and in the latter part of the chapter, Peter began preaching about Jesus. This is what resulted in 5,000 men believing in the Lord Jesus (see Acts 4:4). It also resulted in the arrest of the two apostles.

Peter and John were then brought before the Sanhedrin and asked, "By what power or by what name have you done this?" (Acts 4:7). And that, of course, gave Peter another opportunity to testify of Jesus. And soon, the Sanhedrin

dismissed them under a strong caution not to speak or "teach in the name of Jesus" (Acts 4:17).

Once released, the two apostles went to "their own companions and reported all that the chief priests and elders had said to them" (Acts 4:23). And this is where Psalm 2 comes in. I love this part. Let's read Acts 4:24–26:

> So when they heard that, they raised their voice to God with one accord and said: "Lord, You are God, who made heaven and earth and the sea, and all that is in them, who by the mouth of Your servant David have said: 'Why did the nations rage, and the people plot in vain things? The kings of the earth took their stand, and the rulers were gathered together against the LORD and against His Christ.'"

Basically, their prayer tells us that they saw Psalm 2 happening in their day. They had the revelation of Jesus being set in as King through the resurrection and ascension—that God was setting His King on Mount Zion (see Ps 2:6). They recognized the connection between Herod, Pontius Pilate, along with the Gentiles and the people of Israel setting themselves against Jesus

as what was described in Psalm 2:1–2. They even made the connection to what Peter and John had experienced with a continuation of the raging of the leaders against God's Anointed One. And with that knowledge and understanding, they then prayed,

> Now, Lord, look on their threats, and grant to Your servants that with all boldness they may speak Your word, by stretching out Your hand to heal, and that signs and wonders may be done through the name of Your holy Servant Jesus.
>
> ACTS 4:29

What were they doing here? They were not focusing on the threats of the Sanhedrin or the threats of their adversaries. Instead, they were looking at God. And what happened next was powerful. "And when they had prayed, the place where they were assembled was shaken; and they were all filled with the Holy Spirit, and they spoke the word of God with boldness" (Acts 4:31).

I believe this kind of praying is coming back because we're recovering Psalm 2. There is an

apostolic reality that is coming back to the Church. It's an ancient reality that's teaching us how to pray in this hour. We're not victims, running from the cultural wars, political wars, or international wars. No, we're engaging with God in a new intensity, intentionality, and focus. And God is going to answer our prayers with a fresh outpouring of His Spirit, a fresh anointing on the proclamation of the gospel, and a spirit of revival.

Psalm 2:9 says, "You shall break them with a rod of iron; You shall dash them to pieces like a potter's vessel." I want to tell you that God wants to release His Word like a rod. He wants to release it in your home. He wants to release victorious praying again in your home as He did in mine so that, when you pray, your home is shaken, and all inside are filled with the Holy Spirit. Then that boldness will come to partici-pate—to take the gospel to your neighbors and to the nations—causing your personal story to be connected to God's global storyline in the earth. It's simply part of becoming a Nasharite.

---

1. Jesus said, "Is it not written, 'My house shall be called a house of prayer for all nations'?" (Mark 11:17).

CHAPTER 3
REVIVAL OF BIBLICAL PROPORTIONS

At the very core of the Nasharites is revival. I want to give you a definition of revival because too often people reduce revival to something that it's not. A few people get saved, a few more receive the baptism of the Holy Spirit, and someone receives healing, and many start saying, "Oh, that's revival! God is moving by His Spirit." Don't get me wrong. I love witnessing people being touched by God and coming into a greater relationship with Him. That's wonderful. But a true revival is something more than that.

Revival is when God openly manifests the rule of His Son by the outpouring of the Holy Spirit and the release of apostolic preaching. It's when the Word of God goes forth in such power that demons are cast

out, sicknesses are healed, the powers of darkness are shaken in a region and broken to their core as the Spirit breaks through with the Word. What I'm talking about is the restored power on the preaching of the Word of God.

ACTS 4 FALLOUT

We looked at Acts 4 in our second chapter, how the early church prayed in one accord after Peter and John were released. If you'll recall, they prayed portions from Psalm 2, and then we are told that, when they prayed, "the place where they were assembled together was shaken," they were filled afresh with the Holy Spirit, "and they spoke the word of God with boldness" (Acts 4:31).

The apostles, then, received ability to boldly speak God's Word. But that's not the only result of their prayer. Verse 33 tells us, "And with great power the apostles gave witness to the resurrection of the Lord Jesus. And great grace was upon them all." Now, that's what I want to highlight here. There was a power to preach. It was a grace, a divine enabling, for the apostles to give witness.

In the next chapter, we're given evidence of the kind of power that was let loose. Ananias and Sapphira sold some land, conceived a plan to keep some of the money and hide that fact from the apostles, and then brought the remainder of the profit, laying "it at the apostles' feet" (Acts 5:1–3). This resulted in the husband and wife being carried out, dead! Why? Because they lied to the Holy Spirit (see Acts 5:3). "So great fear came upon all those who heard these things" (Acts 5:5).

The apostles worked miracles, signs, and wonders (see Acts 5:12). Multitudes were added to the church daily (see Acts 5:13–14). The sick were brought "from the surrounding cities to Jerusalem," and they rested on their sickbeds out in the streets in the hope that Peter's shadow going over them as he walked by would heal them (Acts 5:15). Jerusalem as well as the regions surrounding it experienced revival.

There was, however, great fallout from the apostolic preaching. The apostles were thrown into prison because they had continued to preach about Jesus, but "at night an angel of the Lord opened the prison doors and brought them out" (Acts 5:17–19). Even though the apostles were

beaten, they continued to teach and preach that Jesus was the Christ, the Son of God (see Acts 5:40–42). And their preaching had great effect.

When we look at historical revivals like the First and Second Great Awakenings, the impact of the preaching of God's Word in those revivals was the same as the impact the early church apostles had in preaching the Word in their day. *It's very important as a Nasharite to know what revival looks like, to recognize true revival is of biblical proportions. It impacts the teaching and the preaching of the Word.* Not only does the sharing of the gospel come forth with authority and power, resulting in miracles and salvations—and followed by signs and wonders—but the adversary resists and fights against it. He will stir up the hearts of people and leaders, causing them to conspire against Jesus. Remember, Satan doesn't want Jesus to receive His inheritance.

THE DNA OF THE NASHARITES

There are three chapters in the Bible that I would say show us the DNA or characteristics of the Nasharite: Psalm 2, Isaiah 40, and Isaiah 62. I've already walked with you through Psalm 2. And in it, we discovered two important Nasharite traits. Let's review them before we move into the other two chapters.

The first is receiving your identity as a son or daughter of God. Knowing you're a son or daughter who is loved and accepted in the heart of the Father—that you've been adopted by Him —is powerful as it relates to intimacy with Him and authority in prayer. Romans 8:15 tells us, "For you did not receive the spirit of bondage again to fear, but you received the Spirit of adop-

tion by whom we cry out, 'Abba, Father.'" This is the first work of the spirit of prayer—your saying, "Abba, Father, I belong to You." It's the belonging that brings you into the house of prayer and lifts the ceiling of religion so that you can ask for your inheritance in the Father's house. See, religion lies to you and says that you have to do something to earn God's love.

The second characteristic we see illustrated in Psalm 2 is your greatest place of warfare becomes your greatest place of inheritance. You may have chaos, confusion, and rage breaking out in your home. Your marriage may be on the brink of collapse. Your finances may be a mess. You may even be walking through the shadow of death, and the devil wants to drag you down, ensnaring you in the anger, anxiety, questions, and grief of the first heavens. But God wants to teach you how to ascend into the third heaven where you are seated with Him. That's Nasharite DNA right there!

Psalm 2 taught me how to fight. It taught me how to pray. It taught me all about perspective in intercession. But that was only the beginning.

ISAIAH 40 FORERUNNER

Isaiah 40 depicts for us the forerunner spirit or nature of the Nasharite. The only time we see the word *forerunner* in the Bible is in Hebrews 6:20, where it speaks of Jesus entering behind the veil and forerunning into the Holy of Holies in heaven for us. As our Forerunner, He secured our place in the throne room. The nature of the forerunner ministry on the earth was also exemplified for us in the life and ministry of John the Baptist.

John was sent one short step ahead of the first coming of Jesus. He was Jesus' cousin and was the first person to recognize who Jesus was. Amazingly, John did that in his mother's womb: "And it happened, when Elizabeth heard the greeting of Mary, that the babe leaped in her womb; and Elizabeth was filled with the Holy Spirit" (Luke 1:41).

Furthermore, John the Baptist, as we're told in John 1:6–7, was sent from God "for a witness, to bear witness of the Light, that all through him might believe." Verse 8 clarifies for us that John was not the Light "but was sent to bear witness of that Light." John the Baptist came as a fore-

runner to Jesus, preaching a message of repentance and preparation. The plan of his forerunning was to get everyone ready, through the baptism of repentance, to receive Jesus when He came.

The very nature of the forerunner is to take all the hits early and to make a straight path for the coming King. How does that fit in with the DNA of the Nasharites? Well, it requires Nasharites to labor in the place of prayer and fasting before the Lord's return, winning the battle in the heavenlies so that people are ready for His return.

This is the thing about forerunners. They never really fit in. God makes forerunners to be different. They have a prophetic sense or prophetic spirit that they carry. And there's something about their senses, or should I say sensitivities; they're always feeling things at a heightened or deeper level. And they can even seem out of place in their current context. Prophetic people, prophetic intercessors, or forerunning Nasharites seem to run on a different time clock. *Forerunners are living tomorrow, today.* And it creates a tension in their lives. Seeming out of step with the world and spending a lot of time on their own in prayer can give rise to them feeling misunderstood or very

lonely, leaving them vulnerable to attacks by the enemy.

Therefore, it's very important for forerunners to understand all of these things come with the territory. And *they must learn the uncharted territory and terrain before them, somehow carving out a way to help other people through who are coming right behind them.* It's "the voice of one crying in the wilderness: 'Prepare the way of the LORD; make straight in the desert a highway for our God'" (Isa 40:3).

What is a forerunner doing? *A forerunner is building infrastructure in a place that doesn't have any —in a place that seems far removed from civilization!*

As forerunners, Nasharites build highways in the desert for God. They exalt the valleys and raze the mountains. They straighten out the crooked places and smooth the rough. That explains why, as I like to say, *their foreheads are rocks, and their hearts are butter.* The hard-headedness is necessary for changing the landscape before them in prayer, and the tenderheartedness is necessary for relationship with the Father and caring for people.

Nasharites must clear the way and know when it's time to do so. *Nasharite forerunners have a stub-*

bornness about them—the stubbornness of an intercessor —because they know what God has said and what He wants to do, and they simply won't move off it or shy away from it. It's a holy stubbornness like Ezekiel had. God said to Ezekiel, "Like adamant stone, harder than flint, I have made your forehead; do not be afraid of them, nor be dismayed at their looks, though they are a rebellious house" (Ezek 3:9).

What's the purpose for all this rock-headedness and building? It's to prepare the way for the coming glory of the Lord: "The glory of the LORD shall be revealed, and all flesh shall see it together; for the mouth of the LORD has spoken" (Isa 40:5).

When you know the will of God is to bring His glorious salvation to your home and deliverance to your family, and healing in your relationships and breakthrough in your finances, you will not get off the wall of intercession, but your heart will remain tender and responsive to God. The children of God could not inherit the Promised Land because they had hearts hardened by unbelief (Heb 3:19). *Nasharites want rock solid foreheads and tender, believing hearts so that those who come after them can receive their promise.*

If you're going to prepare highways for glory in your home, it's going to take resolve. It's going to take holy stubbornness. You're going to need a supernatural faithfulness that is not about you and your willpower but is about the will of God that has apprehended you until what God has declared is manifested in your home. And that resolve to not back off prayer until you see what it is you've been believing for is the work of God inside you, and it's the nature of the forerunner ministry seen in Isaiah 40 and in the life of John the Baptist.

We must remember, however, that intercession is not convincing God to do something. *Intercession is God convincing you He wants to do something.* And that's what you hold on to in faith, and it's also what holds on to you in the wilderness. The call of God to intercede will fuel your prayer and forerunning work in the wilderness. And so will the knowledge and majesty of God.

We need to get a bigger view of God. That's what Isaiah 40 calls for—a bigger view of God's power, His ability, His greatness, His humility, His love, His wisdom, and His glory. I call it *the unapproachability and approachability of God.* We read about it in the questions God leveled in Isaiah 40:12–14,

18, and 21. When God asks questions in the Bible, He's not looking for answers. He knows the answers before He even asks the questions. *His questions are His interrogations of us and our knowledge of Him.* But as we soon find out in verse 22, it is God "who sits above the circle of the earth, and its inhabitants are like grasshoppers." And it's the knowledge of God that lowers the mountains of pride, arrogance, and self-sufficiency.

The mountains are the stalwart arrogant places in our family—the pride and the resistance. And when you see the mountains of pride in your home, your church, your city, or your region, don't go after the pride. Instead, begin to call the majesty of God to manifest. It's the Isaiah 64:1 cry, "Oh, that You would rend the heavens! That You would come down! That the mountains might shake at Your presence." And then you can begin to declare the greatness, power, and holiness of God to shake every mountain of arrogance.

We go higher as Nasharites, beloved. Our fight isn't "against flesh and blood" (Eph 6:12). It's not against people. But it is "against principalities, against powers, against rulers of the darkness of

this age, against spiritual hosts of wickedness in the heavenly places" (Eph 6:12). So, you need to look up. You must "lift up your eyes on high, and see" your Creator—your majestic God (Isa 40:26).

By the way, don't try to find the names of principalities and powers. Just learn to ascend to the third heaven and become a third heaven warrior who learn how to battle spiritual warfare, not by trying to name an ancient principality, not by trying to uproot it from your wilderness, but by declaring the majesty of God over those rulers and spiritual hosts.

One other thing about forerunners is they must learn to live in the hiddenness of the desert. *God does His greatest work in hiddenness. He does His greatest work when no one knows what's happening.*

The wilderness is a wilderness of romance. It's where you experience God's love and power. You find His affection sustains you. In fact, you learns how to dwell alone with God there and receive your sustenance from Him. It's in the wilderness where God transitions your sources from everything you see to that which is unseen. In the wilderness, you "wait on the Lord" to renew your strength, mounting "up with wings like eagles,"

running and not growing weary, and walking and not fainting (Isa 40:30–31). It's here "He gives power to the weak" (Isa 40:29).

There is supernatural ability to run and never wear out. If we endeavor to wait on the Lord in our own strength, we will get worn out as we keep coming down to the first heavens and trying to fix everything. It's in the third heaven where God wants to bring you into a supernatural place of rest and confidence. It's in your weakness that His "strength is made perfect" and His "grace is sufficient for you" so you can continue to wait and watch (2 Cor 12:9).

ISAIAH 62 WATCHMAN

If you were to ask me, "Where is the Nasharite army in the Bible?" I would say it's Isaiah 62:6–7,

> I have set watchmen on your walls, O Jerusalem; they shall never hold their peace day or night. You who make mention of the Lord, do not keep silent, and give Him no rest till He establishes and till He makes Jerusalem a praise in the earth.

Nasharites are watchmen for Israel. It's part of their DNA.

In 2021, the Lord began to stir something within Dana. She attended a women's conference titled, "Women at the Well," on a Friday evening. Something happened that night that began a great change in her life. When she went to bed that night, she heard the Lord say to her, "Dana, do you love Me?" It's the same question Jesus asked Peter three times in John 21:15–17. And her response was *yes*. In her heart, she knew the Lord was offering her a line to recommission her.

The next morning, Dana and I went to church at Upperroom in Dallas, and Lou Engle stood up to speak. It happened to be the morning when Jews around the world, both secular and religious, were crying out for the Messiah to return. So, Lou asked those present to fill the vacuum of intercession by asking the Lord to reveal Himself to Israel as Messiah. He commissioned us that morning to cry out to God for a revival among Jews throughout the world.

I was sitting next to Dana when Lou went into intercession, and the next thing I knew, Dana fell forward. I mean she fell forward on her face to the floor. For the next three to four hours, she

was in travail. She cried, wept, groaned, and wailed. Then Pastor Michael Miller stood up and said, "I really feel like the Lord is bringing people here to the John 21 beach, where Jesus says, 'Do you love Me?' There's a recommissioning going on. There's a reinstating that's going on."

Dana continued in intercession while the rest of us were praying for Israel. Soon, the Lord began talking to her about Isaiah 62:6, regarding setting watchmen on Israel's walls. A few weeks after this experience, she was in a friend's home when she had another encounter, and in this one she actually saw the army of intercessors. It was in this season where Dana was wrecked by these encounters with the Lord and His recommissioning her that I felt it was time to issue the call to Nasharites. It was time to blow the trumpet and begin to set intercessors on the wall. That was February of 2021, and we had our first Nasharite conference in November of that same year.

Looking at the opening verse of Isaiah 62, "For Zion's sake I will not hold My peace, and for Jerusalem's sake I will not rest," we see a conviction of heart for intercession. Intercessors are not people who try to scream and manipulate God

into getting Him to do what they want. *Interces-sors are consumed with the will of God.* When you are consumed with the will of God and are possessed with the zeal of God, His intercession becomes your intercession. Remember, you're not trying to convince Him to do something. He's convincing you that He wants to do something.

And when we look at Isaiah 62:1, we see the source of the watchman's zeal as "Zion's sake." God Himself said He would not hold His peace "until her righteousness goes forth as brightness, and her salvation as the lamp that burns" (Isa 62:1). In Zechariah 8:2, God said, "I am zealous for Zion with great zeal; with great fervor I am zealous for her." This is how fervent, passionate, and zealous God is for Israel. You can hear His loving and intercessory heart for His people, especially in the following verses:

> The Gentiles shall see your righteousness, and all kings your glory. You shall be called by a new name, which the mouth of the LORD will name. You shall also be a crown of glory in the hand of the LORD, and a royal diadem in the hand of your God. You shall no longer be termed Forsaken, nor shall your land any more be termed Desolate; but you shall be called

Hephzibah, and your land Beulah; for the
LORD delights in you, and your land shall be
married.

ISAIAH 62:2–4

It's apparent that God wants to do something,
and we can think, *Well, why don't You just do it then,
Father?* But His answer to us is that He needs
agreement with His will in heaven to see it estab-
lished in the earth. From the very opening of
Isaiah 62, we are told God is not resting until He
has watchmen stationed on the walls of Israel.
He will not do this alone. He wants Nasharites,
intercessors who share His holy heart, His deep
longings and zeal, to labor with Him to see His
will manifested on earth.

Perhaps you wonder why He feels this way about
Israel. It's because God made covenant with a
man a long time ago by the name of Abraham.
God promised childless Abraham that He would
make Abraham "a great nation" and would give
him a land (Gen 12:1–3). Furthermore, God said
all the the earth would be blessed by Abraham.

In Genesis 15, God then made a covenant with
Abraham that God Himself would fulfill. God

promised Abraham an heir, offspring as numerous as the stars, and land. "When God made a promise to Abraham, because He could swear by no one greater, He swore by Himself" (Heb 6:13). That covenant is still being fulfilled, and that's why we must continue to pray until all the promises in that covenant come to pass.

We're going to take time in the next chapter to really understand God's heart for Israel and the purposes for her and us, the Church, in the last days. But for now, you need to understand the DNA of the Nasharites includes a beloved identity, a third heaven perspective, a forerunning spirit, and a zealous watchfulness for Israel. *God wants to set Nasharites as Isaiah 62 watchmen for Israel—watchmen who won't keep silent until Jerusalem is a praise in all the earth.*

CHAPTER 5
CONNECTED TO ISRAEL'S STORYLINE

I saiah 62:1 tells us what God is after—why He will neither hold His peace nor rest. He desires Jerusalem's righteousness and salvation. Jerusalem will receive her righteousness the same way we receive ours—through faith in Jesus, Yeshua, as Messiah. When we study the Scriptures, we discover her receiving Jesus as Messiah as a nation is connected to the second coming.

One of the names of God is Jehovah Tsidkenu, which means the Lord our righteousness. When we put faith in the death and resurrection of Jesus, the Bible says it is imputed to us as the very righteousness of God (see Rom 4:24). A day is coming when what God does for us individually will be done for an entire nation. Yes, Israel

will be born again in a day. We will see Zion receive Jesus as Messiah, and His righteousness will be imputed and imparted to her (see Rom 11:25–27). Her people will become the remnant, and Mount Zion will become the seat of the throne of God in the age to come. Jesus will rule forever from that throne. This is what God is going to do, and this is what He wants us as intercessors to become gripped with—the salvation and righteousness of Israel. *Nasharites are called to participate in the prophetic storyline of Israel becoming reality.*

WHY ISRAEL?

I began to answer this question in the last chapter. It all goes back to the covenant that God made with Abraham. But let's look at the greater storyline. Let's go back to the beginning.

In Genesis 3, we read about the temptation from the serpent and the fall of Adam and Eve. God pronounced judgment over the serpent and then Adam and Eve. He said to the serpent, "I will put enmity between you and the woman, and between your seed and her Seed; He shall bruise your head, and you shall bruise His heel" (Gen 3:15). Notice the "s" in the seed of Satan isn't

capitalized while the "S" in the Seed of the woman is. The Seed that was to come through the woman would be Jesus, He would be born of a long family line, and He would redeem people from their sin.

In Genesis 11, we read the story of Babel when humanity endeavored to build a tower to the heavens. God stopped them and scattered them by confusing their language. With the story of Babel, the question arose of how God would redeem the nations—and even the earth.

In the very next chapter, Genesis 12, God spoke to a man named Abram, who was living in modern-day Iraq. He told Abram, "Get out of your country, from your family and from your father's house, to a land that I will show you" (Gen 12:1). In the very next verse, God promised Abram that He would make him "a great nation," and in verse 3, God vowed, "And in you all the families of the earth shall be blessed." So, God promised three things: (1) to give Abram land, (2) to make of him a great nation, and (3) to bless all the earth through him.

Next, in Genesis 15, God made covenant with Abram/Abraham as we talked about in our chapter about the Nasharite DNA. And we know

that God would be the One to bring about the promise of a son to Abraham and his wife, Sarah, in their old age, thus birthing the nation of Israel through them.

As the story continued, Abraham begat Isaac, and Isaac begat Jacob, whose name was later changed to Israel after Jacob wrestled with God (see Gen 32:22–28). Israel then had 12 sons through two wives and their respective maidservants. And toward the end of his life, we find Israel prophesying over each of his boys (see Gen 49). When Israel came to Judah, he said, "The scepter shall not depart from Judah, nor a lawgiver from between his feet, until Shiloh comes" (Gen 49:10). Here we see the promise of the Messiah who will be a king. The coming Seed spoken of in God's judgment against Satan will be the King who rules the tribe of Judah.

After being led by the patriarchs like Abraham and Moses, God gave them judges to care for the great many people known as Israel. But the people became dissatisfied with their leaders, and they wanted to be like other nations who had a king (see 1 Sam 8:6). God gave them what they wanted. That was Saul (see 1 Sam 9:17). He failed to obey God's instructions through His

prophet Samuel, and so God selected another—a king "after His own heart" (1 Sam 13:14). His name was David. And David became the king to whom God said, "You shall not fail to have a man sit before Me on the throne of Israel" (1 Kgs 8:25). The Messiah will be the Son of David. He will sit on David's throne and rule over the house of Jacob forever.

Jesus was born the Son of Abraham, the Son of David. Through all Israel's failures and weaknesses, faithful prophets and intercessors—like Isaiah, Jeremiah, Ezekiel, and Daniel—came forward at strategic points in her history to keep her storyline progressing to the day when the Seed was born.

Jesus did come to the nation of Israel, being born in Bethlehem and raised in Nazareth. For 30 years, Jesus was relatively hidden, and then for three and a half years, He was revealed as He ministered among His people. He came to the lost sheep of Israel, teaching in the synagogues, performing miracles and wonders in front of crowds gathered around Him, healing the sick, and raising the dead. He called the Twelve and sent them out to preach the gospel, heal the sick, raise the dead, and work miracles. And

though some believed, many rejected Him as Messiah.

It's no wonder Jesus lamented over Israel, over Jerusalem. He said,

> O Jerusalem, Jerusalem, the one who kills the prophets and stones those who are sent to her! How often I wanted to gather your children together, as a hen gathers her chicks under her wings, but you were not willing! See! Your house is left to you desolate; for I say to you, you shall see Me no more till you say, "Blessed is He who comes in the name of the LORD!"
>
> MATTHEW 23:37–39

Jesus was quoting from Psalm 118:26 when He said, "Blessed is He who comes in the name of the LORD!" He was telling those around Him and all Israel that they would not see Him again until they received Him as their Messiah. In a way, Jesus was boxing Himself into a corner, and it provoked the rage of Satan to completely destroy Israel so that her people would never cry for Him to return as her Messiah.

As Israel's story continued, Jesus was betrayed by Judas and arrested (see Matt 26:14, 47–50). Jesus appeared before the Sanhedrin and then Pontius Pilate. He was scourged and mocked and crucified. But death couldn't hold Him. He was resurrected from the dead and then spent 40 days on earth, teaching on the Kingdom of God.

Jesus was asked by the disciples in Acts 1:6, "Lord, will You at this time restore the kingdom to Israel?" And He responded:

> It is not for you to know times or season which the Father has put in His own authority. But you shall receive power when the Holy Spirit has come upon you; and you shall be witnesses to Me in Jerusalem, and in all Judea and Samaria, and to the end of the earth.

> ACTS 1:7–8

Though they didn't know when, the disciples understood by Jesus' teaching and the words of the prophets that there was a day coming when Jesus would restore the kingdom of Israel. There would be a time when every one of the promises God made throughout the narrative of the nation would be fulfilled, including those He made to

Abraham. Jesus knew for the season that remained before His second coming they would need the fire of God upon their lives. And that fire they received in the upper room on the Day of Pentecost. It would break out from Jerusalem, Judea, Samaria, even to the ends of the earth. It would touch the Gentiles. It would break through every barrier, bond, or boundary. And what we've seen for the last 2,000 years is the expansion of what Jesus promised those fishermen and what God promised Abraham and Israel before them.

All of this is why Israel's existence and storyline matters. As the apostle Paul explained, "But through [Israel's] fall, to provoke them to jealousy, salvation has come to the Gentiles," and when "the fullness of the Gentiles has come in," Jesus will return, and "all Israel will be saved" (Rom 11:11, 25–27).

THE NASHARITE CONNECTION

The calling of the Nasharite is a calling to cry out to God for Israel to come to salvation. I believe God is raising up a global upper room in which Nasharites will be spiritually set upon the walls of Jerusalem to cry out to God to bring forth

salvation for Israel. We are to cry out that the blindness over the people of Israel would be broken off—that the veil would be torn away—so they would receive Yeshua as Messiah. We don't want to keep Jesus solely in our nice Gentile homes in our nice little Gentile worlds. No, it's time to be struck to the heart of how "their fall" has been "riches for the world, and their failure riches for [us] the Gentiles" (Rom 11:12).

Beloved, there are some destructive heresies and false doctrines within the Church that we must rid ourselves of and get complete clarity on God's Word and heart and purposes for Israel. I want to say it very clearly: *The Church does not replace Israel.* There are doctrines out there that espouse the Church has inherited all the promises made to Israel in her stead, and now God is done with Israel. Nothing could be further from the truth. The first verse of Romans 11 completely rejects that idea. Paul wrote, "I say then, has God cast away His people? Certainly not! For I also am an Israelite, of the seed of Abraham, of the tribe of Benjamin. God has not cast away His people whom He foreknew."

As a matter of fact, we discover that what Paul dealt with in Romans 11 was arrogance—the

arrogance of the Gentiles. If we're ignorant, he said, concerning God's heart and plan for Israel, then we will become arrogant. *Ignorance breeds arrogance.* And we don't want to be arrogant. We want to be humble and grateful. Rather than being arrogant, Paul taught that we should fear God—to "consider the goodness and severity of God" (Rom 11:20, 22).

We should be thankful for the role Israel has played in our being grafted in. For we were "once disobedient to God, yet have now obtained mercy through their disobedience, even so these also have now been disobedient, that through the mercy shown" us "they also may obtain mercy" (Rom 11:30–31). We want to understand and be unified with these purposes of God.

Let me state this very clearly. God is raising up a Nasharite army of hidden intercessors. *The narrative of our lives as Nasharites is connected to the biblical, prophetic storyline of Israel and the Lord's return.* We must get this. I understand all too well how difficult it can be to understand the significance, value, and purpose of interceding for the nation and people of Israel. I sat in prayer meetings for years—what were boring prayer meetings for me —before I grasped why it was important to do

what I was doing. I was praying out of obedience because the Bible tells us to "pray for the peace of Jerusalem: 'May they prosper who love you'" (Ps 122:6). What I discovered after time was I was not only connecting to the storyline of Israel, but I was actually connecting to something even bigger—the heart of God and His plan for the ages.

My prayer is that the Spirit of revelation hits you concerning where this all is headed. And here it is: Jesus is going to return, and when Israel, the remnant, is backed into a corner as the antichrist army is almost about to destroy her, at that moment, what is written in Zechariah 14:2–4 will happen.

> For I will gather all the nations to battle against Jerusalem; the city shall be taken, the houses rifled, and the women ravished. Half of the city shall go into captivity, but the remnant of the people shall not be cut off from the city. Then the LORD will go forth and fight against those nations as He fights in the day of battle. And in that day His feet will stand on the Mount of Olives, which faces Jerusalem on the east.

Jesus will destroy the antichrist army, and He will cut a path, a valley, so that the remnant can escape. Then Jesus

> will pour on the house of David and on the inhabitants of Jerusalem the Spirit of grace and supplication; then they will look on [Him] whom they pierced. Yes, they will mourn for Him as one mourns for his only son.
>
> ZECHARIAH 12:10

That's the day the apostle Paul pointed to in Romans 11—the day when the remnant of the nation is saved. And do you know what that's going to release? It's going to release life from the dead for the whole world. And that's going to usher in the millennial reign of Jesus. We will see the glory of God and the reversal of the curse. We will see the utter destruction of Satan and his tyranny. The removal, even, of the effects of darkness and wickedness and sin will happen as Jesus' throne is placed on this earth in Jerusalem.

Like no other time in world history, we are seeing things being set in order for the Lord's return. We are seeing nations raging against Israel and against the Lord's Anointed. World

leaders are conspiring in this hour against a small plot of land the size of the state of New Jersey. The rage of Satan has spewed through the centuries to wipe that nation off the face of the earth. The devil rages at the places where and the people with whom God has made for Himself. But God has kept Israel, and He is keeping her this very day.

Jesus is still weeping over Jerusalem. He wants to bring friends into His weeping and travailing heart for Israel. He is calling Nasharites and setting them as watchmen all over the earth. These Nasharites are simple folk like us, Gentiles who have connected to the heart of God and care about what He cares about. He is granting to us a spirit of prayer whereby we will not rest until He establishes and makes Jerusalem a praise in all the earth (see Isa 62:7).

THE WORD & AUTHORITY IN PRAYER

I had mentioned in chapter 2 about living in Psalm 2 for a year and a half. If you'll recall, I said in passing that I had also focused on Psalm 1 in that difficult season after our son, Nash, went to be with the Lord. I want to look at Psalm 1 with you because His Word is what powers our intercession. *We find words to pray coming out of the intimacy of abiding in His Word.* This is essential for you as a Nasharite.

Psalm 1 contains revelation that shifted my life, and it's absolutely critical to having authority in prayer. Let's look at the beginning:

> Blessed is the man who walks not in the counsel of the ungodly, nor stands in the path of sinners, nor sits in the seat of the scornful;

> but his delight is in the law of the LORD, and in His law he meditates day and night. He shall be like a tree planted by the rivers of water, that brings forth its fruit in its season, whose leaf also shall not wither; and whatever he does shall prosper.

PSALM 1:1–3

Authority in prayer comes when words come out of your mouth that were born or breathed from God. When you come out from under the counsel of the ungodly, remove yourself from the path of sinners, move away from the wicked words common in much conversation, and read God's counsel, you begin your journey of falling in love and finding delight in the Word of God.

The enemy has been working overtime over the past decade to direct us away from that which is true, noble, just, pure, lovely, virtuous, and good (see Phil 4:8). He has used the screens of our computers, televisions, phones, and cinemas to plaster our minds with the news of the day and the chatter of society, with the dirty and impure, the worthless and profane. Rather than meditating on things that are "praiseworthy" or of "good report," our minds have been sated with

the evil and ungodly around us (Phil 4:8). All the junk Satan throws at us through social media and the like feeds fear, anxiety, worry, anger, and sin. It stifles the spirit of prayer and the spirit of faith necessary for intercession and godly living.

I think a major tactic of Satan has been to do whatever he can to snuff out the spirit of faith in the Church. But God wants to restore faith to His Church. Romans 10:17 instructs us that "faith comes by hearing, and hearing by the word of God." That's the Romans 10 reality. We must hear the Word of God. It's what we need to hear in order to believe. Nasharites must be intercessors of faith in the promises and Words of God—otherwise, why pray?

We must come out from under the influence of ungodly counsel. We must take the counsel of His Word and learn to delight in the precepts and warnings and commandments that are found therein.

THE ONE THING NEEDED

I'm reminded of Mary of Bethany in Luke 10:39. She made a radical choice to sit at the feet of Jesus. Her sister, Martha, "was distracted with

much serving," and asked Jesus to tell Mary to help her (Luke 10:40). But Mary refused to get caught up in the distractions all around. She chose to listen to the words of Jesus and allow them to go deep into her spirit. Jesus said to Martha, "But one thing is needed, and Mary has chosen that good part, which will not be taken away from her" (Luke 10:42).

Fast forward to Mary's next season, and we find her brother, Lazarus, has died. They had requested Jesus come, but Jesus stayed two more days where He was (see John 11:3–6). When Jesus finally came, Mary waited while Martha ran out immediately, saying to Him, "Lord, if You had been here, my brother would not have died," and then they proceeded to have what reads more like a theological discussion (John 11:20–27).

Afterward, Martha told Mary that Jesus asked for her, so Mary went to Jesus and "fell down as His feet, saying to Him, 'Lord, if You had been here, my brother would not have died'" (John 11:32). They were the same words that Martha said to Jesus. But something happened when Jesus saw her weeping. John 11:33 says, "He groaned in the spirit and was troubled." Jesus was moved by the

tears of the one who had chosen to sit at His feet and let His words soak into the depths of her heart.

As you sit before God's Word—letting His words descend into your deep—something happens so that, when the hour of crisis comes in your world, a prayer arises from your deep that calls out to His deep. And that, beloved, pulls resurrection power out of Him. This is what happened in John 11 that led to the resurrection of Lazarus.

We need a Psalm 1 generation that can come out of the counsel of the ungodly, off the path of sinners and the seat of all the haters, and fall madly in love with the Word of God and the God of the Word. We need Nasharites like Mary of Bethany—men and women who sit at the feet of Jesus and "delight in the law of the Lord" (Ps 1:2). We need Nasharites who "meditate day and night" in God's law (Ps 1:2).

Do you love the Word of God? Do you enjoy reading it and meditating on it? I have experienced seasons where my love for the Word was abounding. But I've also known seasons where it wasn't. Enjoying His Word is our inheritance.

Here's the secret: *The spirit of prayer is the anointing resting on the life that's abiding in the Word of God.*

THE POWER OF THE WORD

There are various descriptions given in Scripture for the Word of God. The Lord asked the prophet Jeremiah, "'Is not My word like a fire?' says the LORD, "and like a hammer that breaks the rock in pieces" (Jer 23:29). And in Hebrews 4:12, we're told,

> For the word of God is living and powerful, and sharper than any two-edged sword, piercing even to the division of soul and spirit, and of joints and marrow, and is a discerner of the thoughts and intents of the heart.

Fire, hammer, two-edged sword, living, powerful, piercing—these are words used to help us understand the power and might of the Word of God. His Word is a force to be reckoned with. It's what Jesus spoke to overcome temptation in the wilderness. And it's the Word we need to replace our weak words in prayer and intercession.

God wants to anoint you with a spirit of prayer for revival because it's that kind of prayer that

breaks the power of the devil. *Praying His Word in faith that rises out of the intimacy of relationship with Jesus possesses an authority that brings power-packing results.* God wants to release His Word in your life, in your home, and in your family like a battering ram. He wants to break off generational iniquities. He was to tear down demonic assignments in your home by the power of His Word.

Ask God to grip you with a hunger and love for His Word. Ask Him to then grip your heart for revival and for the salvation of Israel. Let Him take the weak words of your mouth and turn them into the battering ram of His Word. Ask Him for your inheritance.

CHAPTER 7
ASKING FOR YOUR INHERITANCE

L ooking again at the third part of the drama in Psalm 2, we watch the Father behold His beautiful Son in eternity. He said to Jesus, "You are My Son, today I have begotten You" (Ps 2:7). And then He said, "Ask of Me" (Ps 2:8). This was an invitation to Jesus the Son to make eye contact with the Father and to make His request of the Father. This, beloved, is an invitation to us.

When the Lord said to me, "Corey, come out of the shadows. Make eye contact with Me. Get secure in My affections for you as your Father," something happened. The religious ceiling lifted, and I could see my inheritance. For years, I couldn't see it. I wasn't sure if my family and I were going to make it through what felt like

unbearable and never-ending grief. We were in survival mode, trying to get through the rage and chaos and confusion. I was just fighting it, but when I came into the confidence of His affection for me as His son, I was assured that God and I made up the majority.

I want you to know that you and God are the majority. I don't care how many enemies are against you. I don't care how deep the debt is. I don't care how deep the addiction is. I don't care how impossible the situation is. You and God are the majority. And in that place, the religious ceiling will lift, and you will begin to see your inheritance.

Listen to the words of the Father to you: "Ask of Me, and I will give You the nations for Your inheritance, and the ends of the earth for Your possession" (Ps 2:8). This will birth the Nasharite reality in your soul. It's your inheritance as the beloved son or daughter of God.

I believe God wants to mark you. He wants to release in you a fresh spirit of faith, a fresh spirit of prayer. And He wants you to ask Him for that which He has spoken to you. *Ask for that which God has promised you. Ask for the place where the enemy raged in the greatest warfare against you.* Let

that be the tipoff to where you need to be living and asking.

WHY ASK?

Asking is the rule of the Kingdom. God is relational. He is conversational. God is into talking with Himself and with us. He is not into a utilitarian transactional exchange devoid of relationship. The Father says, "I'm going to talk to You." Jesus says, "I'm going to declare to you what the Father has said to Me."

That's the secret. The Father speaks first, and then you ask Him what He told you to ask Him. "Ask of Me, and I will give you the nations for Your inheritance." And that is the revelation of intercession—the revelation of the spirit of prayer. *The spirit of prayer for revival is rooted in intimacy.* It's rooted in conversation. It's rooted in eye contact. It's rooted in communion. It's rooted in fellowship.

The Father has designed you to discover your inheritance as an overflow of intimacy with Him. And He tells you what to ask Him for, and then you ask Him for that as your inheritance. Beloved, this is how God taught me to pray.

As we have discussed, we want to be faithful in prayer for Israel. We want zeal for the salvation of the children of Abraham. But the Father also wants us to ask Him for the nations. And the hour for us to do so is now. J*oin Jesus in asking the Father for His inheritance in your nation.*

God is releasing a spirit of prayer upon the Nasharite army. It's not going to be a bunch of widows who are screaming at an unjust judge. It's going to be confident sons, a confident Bride, standing before a good Father and a righteous Judge to see the breakthrough of God released in their lives.

Whose conversation are you going to buy into? Will you buy into the words of the enemy, "Let us break off Their bonds in pieces"? Will you buy into the adversary's lies and submit to his plan? Or will you buy into the words of your Father? It really does come down to that.

May we be people who drink deeply of the kisses of the Father's Word. *May we be those Nasharites who drink deeply of His affections and out of the overflow begin to ask Him for our inheritance and that of His Son's. This is revival praying.*

CHAPTER 8
A FINAL PICTURE

H ebrews 7:24–25 talks about Jesus as a perpetual Priest—a forever Priest. We read,

> But He, because He continues forever, has an unchangeable priesthood. Therefore He is also able to save to the uttermost those who come to God through Him, since He always lives to make intercession for them.

Right now, Jesus is at the right hand of the Father praying for you. Your name is being mentioned in the throne room of God!

I want you to think about the power of that hidden Man's prayer life on your life. Do you

know Jesus has spent eternity in hiddenness outside of the three and a half years of His manifestation? He was hidden in relative obscurity for 30 years of the 33 that He lived on the earth. But that was as it should have been because I've come to understand that *hiddenness is the glory and the home of the intercessor.*

HIDDENNESS

As a Nasharite, you need to see the glory of being hidden with God in the place of intercession. If you don't understand that, then you'll be frustrated most of the time. You'll walk around with an inner dialogue that questions why you're not impacting more people. But the glory and the mystery of intercession is that it's hidden. It may not immediately impact a lot of people—people you can see or people who can see you. The ramifications and consequences of your prayer life are eternal. They're reaching into eternity, and you can't always know or see how your hidden intercession is making a difference.

I just want to paint you a final picture of what praying in hiddenness as a Nasharite may look like. I've seen how God works with intercessors. 99.9 percent of the Body of Christ will not stand

on stages. That 99.9 percent will not have a million YouTube views or TikTok or Instagram followers. In fact, that 99.9 percent will live with a relatively small sphere of influence. This can cause us to ask, "Is it only about preachers and worship leaders on stages?" The simply answer to that is *no.*

I believe it's about a deeper and more foundational revelation that is absolutely crucial to all intercessors, all Nasharites, and it's this: *There is something greater than being on stages in front of the eyes of men; it's being on the stage before the eyes of the Creator of the universe, knowing that He sees you, He values your voice, and it's your voice that moves Him and dispatches resources into the earth.*

I want to remind you that, if there is one revelation a Nasharite needs to have, it's this: *God hears you, and He answers your prayers.* The truth is, though, it can be difficult to keep hold of that revelation simply because you can succumb to the adversary's devices to look at what's happening in the first heavens and below. But God is faithful to remind you through His Word to look up, to ascend to the third heaven where you're seated with Him.

Whatever God has called you to is on God. But what you can step into is the revelation of the audience that you have with God. *Any other audience—whether it's 3 people or 30,000—is a major step down from talking to God.*

CONSIDER HIM

Hebrews 12:3 commands us to consider Jesus "who endured such hostility from sinners against Himself, lest you become weary and discouraged in your souls." It's always His example that we look to and learn from.

When we look at Jesus' earthly life, we find Him appearing briefly as a baby swaddled and lying in a manger (see Luke 2:7). We see Him at eight days old, being presented in the temple (see Luke 2:21–22). We're told that Simeon held Him, and Anna saw Him there (see Luke 2:28, 38). Then all we're told is "the Child grew and became strong in spirit, filled with wisdom; and the grace of God was upon Him" (Luke 2:40).

We see Him briefly again when He was twelve years old, going with His parents to Jerusalem for the Feast of the Passover (see Luke 2:42). On the

family's return home, He didn't continue with them. He was "missing" for three days (see Luke 2:46). His parents went looking for Him and found Him in the temple, listening to the teachers and even asking them questions. When questioned by His parents about His "disappearance," He said, "Why did you seek Me? Did you not know that I must be about My Father's business?" (Luke 2:49).

Several years passed in Jesus' life that we don't see record of in Scripture. The one thing we know, however, is that He didn't begin His public ministry until He was thirty years old. So, it was not as if Jesus was completely hidden away from everyone, but His true hiddenness was seen in that people didn't know Him as the Son of God. They didn't fully comprehend who He was and what He was telling them would take place.

At thirty, Jesus was baptized by John the Baptist (see Luke 3:21). Then Jesus went into the wilderness—into hiddenness—for forty days (see Luke 4:1–2). He came out of the wilderness and began His ministry, going about doing miracles and telling those healed or delivered not to tell anyone. He would find a secret place away from

the disciples and crowds to pray to the Father (see Luke 4:42). He endeavored stay on mission, moving among crowds and His disciples, yet there was an isolation He experienced because many didn't understand who He really was.

> Then He took the twelve aside and said to them, "Behold, we are going up to Jerusalem, and all things that are written by the prophets concerning the Son of Man will be accomplished. For He will be delivered to the Gentiles and will be mocked and insulted and spit upon. They will scourge Him and kill Him. And the third day He will rise again." But they understood none of these things; this saying was hidden from them, and they did not know the things which were spoken.
>
> LUKE 18:31–34

Before His arrest, Jesus took His disciples to the garden of Gethsemane to pray with Him, but the disciples fell asleep (see Luke 22:39–45). Then Jesus was arrested and sentenced to die on the cross. The disciples scattered, leaving Him. There was a handful who gathered around the cross. Some mocked Him and called Him a fake.

After He was resurrected, He revealed Himself to a few. Yet the impact and the glory of His life has persisted and will persist for eternity.

In all of this, Jesus fulfilled His mission as God's Servant, though He was the Son of God. Isaiah 42:1 says, "Behold! My Servant whom I uphold, My Elect One in whom My soul delights! I have put My Spirit upon Him; He will bring forth justice to the Gentiles." And then in Isaiah 49:2, we read, "And He has made My mouth like a sharp sword; in the shadow of His hand He has hidden Me, and made Me a polished shaft; in His quiver He has hidden Me."

Within these verses, we see a picture of Jesus as the Servant of God, loved by the Father and hidden in the Father's bosom. And the Father places the Spirit upon Him to bring justice, and the Father also chooses the time to pull Jesus out of hiding as a prepared vessel for His day of manifestation.

Consider Jesus. Let Him be your example. God wants to use hiddenness in your life as He used it in Jesus' life. It's one of the core realities of the Nasharite anointing. *Wouldn't you rather be hidden in this age because prayers live forever than to be fully know in this age and never remembered thereafter?*

Let God mark your life as a hidden intercessor, as a Nasharite. It's your glory. Embrace it, and let God use your life as He sees fit to usher in the greatest revival the earth has ever known.

ABOUT THE AUTHOR

Corey Russell's passion is to awaken the Church across the earth to the revelation of Jesus, intimacy with Holy Spirit, and the power of prayer. He has written 9 books, has released 6 prayer albums, and is discipling thousands through his online school at coreyrussellonline.com. Corey is currently on the pastoral team at House Denver. He lives in Denver Colorado with his family.

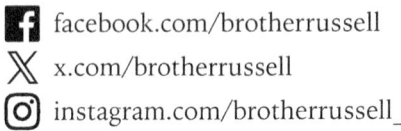

facebook.com/brotherrussell
x.com/brotherrussell
instagram.com/brotherrussell_

ALSO BY COREY RUSSELL

Fellowship of the Burning Heart

Reclaiming Revival: Calling a Generation to Contend for Historic Awakening

The Gift of Tears

Teach Us to Pray: Prayer That Accesses Heaven and Changes Earth

Inheritance: Clinging to God's Promises in the Midst of Tragedy

Prayer: Why Our Words to God Matter

Ancient Paths: Rediscovering Delight in the Word of God

The Glory Within: The Interior Life and the Power of Speaking in Tongues

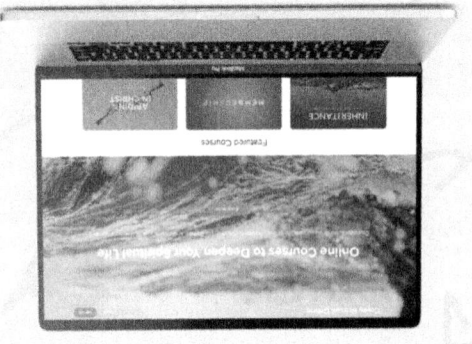

COREY RUSSELL ONLINE

ONLINE COURSES TO DEEPEN YOUR SPIRITUAL LIFE